MW01193802

BONE CONFETTI
Muriel Leung

Noemi Press
Las Cruces, New Mexico

Bone Confetti (c) 2016 by Muriel Leung
All rights reserved. Printed in the United States.

ISBN 978-1-934819-60-9

Cover design by Sarah Gzemski
Interior design by Krystal Languell
Cover art by Kimberly Jones, *Cling*, 2015. Archival pigment print,
        30 x 24 inches. Courtesy of artist.
        http://www.kimberlyreneeart.com/

Library of Congress Cataloging-in-Publication Data

Names: Leung, Muriel, author.
Title: Bone confetti / Muriel Leung.
Description: Las Cruces, NM : Noemi Press, 2016.
Identifiers: LCCN 2016026439 | ISBN 9781934819609 (pbk.)
Classification: LCC PS3612.E9217 A6 2016 | DDC 811/.6--dc23
LC record available at https://lccn.loc.gov/2016026439

Published by Noemi Press, Inc. A Nonprofit Literary Organization
www.noemipress.org

BONE CONFETTI

Muriel Leung

Winner of the 2015 Noemi Press Book Award for Poetry

BONE
CONFETTI

MURIEL
LEUNG

CONTENTS

IN ABSENTIA-LAND: A WEDDING

IN ABSENTIA-LAND: AN EPILOGUE

To my mother, Fei Chin, and all the ghosts who came before us

IN ABSENTIA-LAND:

A ROMANCE

In Absentia-land, we become two tiny terrors in a dead year. Two blitzed countries and the artifact of sleep. In this world I pray: unshutter us. Once, we knew a newness like a wool coat. Now we sharpen our heads against stone—to be sparked back to life. *There, there*, says the tundra. *What do you see?* The primordial singe. Gifted two pairs of marble glass, we lay on a briar bed and place the glass over our eyes. This is how I want to love you—mouth full of cyanide kelp and the words that soot. By way of book and bone, we opt to mimic-pray.

MOURN YOU BETTER

Ecstatic phrase: mourn you better. Or else.
Surrender to the cherry nothingness of go back
to the everyday. Like a runaway gurney I should
lie awake for a pink comet to engulf me. I should
prick myself over and over with a thorn. Its grip
should strike me to grave.

Plenty of things to cry about—

    Afterthought: dead

    Sun and sugarland: dead

    Briar ghost: dead

    Mother: dead

The bones go clacking up the chimney. Time used to

mean, *Let us be better to each other in the now.* Today it means—

Don't wear red on your wedding day.

Suck salt off your thumb.

Don't cry.

Go on. Live without me.

If I paint the suture trees or comb the luminescent
waste or huff the volcanic air. Something monstrous turns
my way but is blanketed in the prettiest lilac down
all gushed in purple-white.

The Lost Years

I was walking along the dandelion path when the cellar door called to me. *Oh pretty noose*, the little darkness said.

The little darkness in the shape of a horse. A horse with a broken buck.

I am making an inventory of all things. The body pulp in mason jars. Something of consequence. An ash of you.

Wake up red. Everything red.

Combing through these spooked years to find a white hair and rotted tooth. The rest of you intact. *Oh good*, one thinks. And then.

Sometimes the specter leaves you flowers. The flowers devolve into smoke. You appreciate the gesture, pour them tea. No one talks about what they have lost.

Garden of Perennial Things

Potential. Noxious word on a thorny spindle.
The future is full of potential, they say, and I
magnify center. A gesture towards love, plain
but incomplete. Never enough water to be had.
This and that strain cannot grow together.

It is this terrible logic that makes me flail harder,
my rind catching dirt and fleas. No one
special in this equation, which is how silence
begets charity—itself not inherently dangerous but needs
the most obvious stitches to bleed, make a cause worthy.
It was charity that thought up bullets instead of seeds.

I was taught to lie on my stomach when dust blows
over me. There is only generous love and when you give,
give up the whole country until there is only *need*
to map the years to come. Need to love you better.

Need to understand: nothing will ever flower in this garden

but thank the shrapnel lodged so deep I can barely feel it.

Hologram Theory

Some things I am learning through the process of light
and how my hand passes through the body screen of you
sitting there with your ham leg
and hyper-clear spacesuit. I love you
and I think sometimes you are the left half
of my terrible beached heart. Its anvil
worth is pleading with the dull whir
of your projection. In many ways, this feels
more real. You insist on the heavy dose of the day
to day remote control dive forward. With this,
I can make you say all the nice things like, *I belong
to your pretty little liver* or, *If you are on fire, I will burn
with you too.* When I want to hold your hand, I just
hold it out towards the peachy static of your
finger tips. You blink to assure me of the viability
of our future in flicker-light revisions. If I can
no longer recall the spiny sensation of you
against my thighs, then I will have to work
harder and think less of the dead,
of you jarred up in crystalline bathwater
while your hologram bright face hovers
across the dinner table. Let's not talk
about that. Today, you are taking on
the origin of the color *blue*, and who decided
on the name *blue* anyway—it is so provincial.
They say we are a vat of tingly particles
moving aimlessly in the caution of our own
waste though sometimes we rest
our fingers on the ghost of a lung
that huffs that other body's good hard air.

Misery Machine

In file by file order, make a mess

  out of grief in the red tumble

machine and the feeling

  ropes in the impenetrable

okay. Pocket-sized ghosts

  in orderly shuffle. The past

on a conveyor belt, in a box

  with pins, laughing along

a tapering path. How stuffed

  with green traps and other

ornamental dangers padding

  the havoc of specters turning

and turning. Bring them

  home now—ship them

to each razed corner of

  a heart I am not afraid

to bite. Through stutter

and howl, blood in the throat,

each feeling identical as

the next and piling at the door.

In the swallow, this clacking

bred into my garden

happily calls this body

house where it lives on and on

in the horror buttons of time.

I Will Find Something to Mourn Today

The quality of mourning like a mammoth
bone hitting the speakers. Teach me how
to be terrified today and meditate on this:
how taut the fingers vine across a starved
navel. Syllabic muse filled with dread.

City of mourners. Their light-up vigilance
sweeping up grief. In the be-good of a tapered
feeling, say, *Stay dead.* I dream of apples
and courage. I bite an apple in the dark.
Note how wolf and veil both adored me.

To mourn close to mourning with thorn
at the chest. Always blood and snow but
no belly to soft. To burn like paper
and lightning tree. Raise me to spark.
Run those ruined fingers through everything.

Happiness Theorem

The plan is to erect a delicious sounding word connoting both joy and pleasure in its ringing. It relies on fashioning first an unstable box that contains within it a goose egg and some troubled verses. The relationship between these disparate objects is symbiotic in that all rely equally on the other to survive if to survive means to make meaning. This is a commendable skill in the schematic rendering of fear operations in the world. To survive at present is no longer birthright but a learned process one acquires through rigorous schooling. Uncertainty opens the attic door to pirating ghosts. Uncertainty lines the bed with metallic devices spliced into brain activity. In its earlier forms uncertainty was a marked derivative of joy making. Time wears on. The connection grows prickly. Joy, more interested in transmogrification in its penchant for contortions and peculiarities, suggests a natural inclination towards uncertainty. The issue is not their likeness but where their tails split. At some point uncertainty subjugates joy and for that reason joy's genetic composition is eternally altered. One does not inherit joy in the same way as their parent. This is to say we all must wear happiness like a disorder we cannot shake.

Robot Pleasure

This is how a serrated blade sinks
its teeth into the world-box. Believe me

and a thousand floating hats. Sky opens here
and candied debris spits from a hung mouth.

How dutifully we perform a robot pleasure
onto one another. Poplar trees awash in radio,

nightmares of blue bombs. A tarred river
bubbles in the speckled lining of my flesh.

Today is new. This is an arm I fashion
out of wool and heartbreak. Sensation cubed.

With adoration and a gray veil, I am wed
and the sordid details of my day are confetti

for someone else's fodder. Though to be touched
past entrails would be nice, the liver licked.

Give me all the feelings and ticking
miracle vial that says: *enchant, enchant.*

As in microwavable hammocks is the answer
to a future without crinkle. Someone weighs

the moon on a finger chart. Someone marries
on the moon. All is lovely made of smashed heads.

IN ABSENTIA-LAND:

A FUNERAL

When I pluck the marbles from my eyes, you are wholly vanished. The spooks watch from stalwart buildings barred with iron. In an upright position, I carry my bag of holes. Funereal noise and then the flock, dressed all in black, feather over me while church bells ring. *Eat, eat,* they say, spooning sugar into my every fold of flesh. *NO WANT,* I mutter. I stitch my mouth shut as each holds one limb of noxious dead over me. *In Absentia*-land, pretend to sleep or join the procession behind the petaling black. I choose this ribbon tossed and frayed edge of godliness. I march by news flying by, which says: *Alive! New day!* The marquee skips.

I Love You, Dead

For such stillness there should be teeth and wine enough
to yank the thought up throat. When she dies, she dies.

She plunges her blood toes into somebody's ash tea. A kindness
and a copper box. In another life, she was a jujube.

I am an overeater. She is not a body I want to eat. Shiny rot
in the forest mulch. Though she stews gently. Her thoughts

of me are always generous. Her thoughts are always mangled
and full of electric suction cups. For example, she wants

to wear my lungs for a bag of pipes. These are the days
of brilliance and poetry. Bloated with salt and our little muses.

My jaw now is a little worse for wear. I need her like a metal
tinge and mechanical throb. Bury her though she leaps up

with cumbersome thirst. She swarms me. She thrusts a hand
upward and through me. Nothing stays. Is knobbed

and oozing past a stone. What heart. What sponge for brain.
She will not fit inside my tiny mouth, my mouth full of dead hair.

Dead Things

When I say dead mouth, language dead.
Dead lovers. I want them to last, but also dead.
Sky is dead, there is no want for light.
So God too is dead beyond the primordial leap.

History dead though terror lives on in digital marquee.
Freedom dead though I have paper and apricots and everything I can eat.
Memory dead (I am forgetting everyday).

Dead was once clever and now it loves the thrill.
Dead in the towers and every skeletal dead.
How lovely the dead chorus gets the flowers.
I will my body to flower but I also—dead.

Of Sound Body and Mind

Sit up! Twinned fates of body and mind—the former sealed in radiant glass.

Straighten out the arch!

The body, a violin that someone is always fingering.

The body, elastic but also put over a cold rock slab. To sharpen.

Diagnosis: the house overturned. I must reconsider how I have been acting.

Sit up! I lay the mind out flat to iron.

Pain—I'll dry it out on a clothesline. To pain the pain.

Take these everyday for the rest of your life.

So what if I go on without song?

Punch the wall. Three round holes.

At the sight of blood, inhale and somersault towards the ER.

It won't do any good anyway.

I keep doing it to myself.

Somewhere in the catacomb, a green will bring me back to life.

MOURN YOU BETTER

I should kiss the electric spark that loves me

but the glassy notion rests in the cancerous region

of a single bone and nothing praised.

But if I let myself be thorough in this undertaking

of dire roses and the tyranny of grass in withering states,

I will learn something new about you.

Something new about you—

    Abbreviated husk in a feral tree

    Your germy motor heart

    Your ever-dead locomotive, happy in the making

None of this is real or else I will climb that

wiry mouth and think: how hung-tired the moon

when the worm tunnels through your fleshy sack.

For now, I will love a drone that pours over me

with shimmery grips of imperfect hands. Delight

in the pummeling sensation and give me all that good

grieving. My little house of sorry. Ready to let

my feeling go for a tincture of some robot infinite.

The Lost Years

Who is hung there by the crystal and chandelier. *I'm still here,* says the hollow madam tilting forward.

You must understand. In this closet is an ocean in a canopy bed. Nothing is what it seems.

Tread carefully the velvet noise of the house's guillotine.

If there is a dead thing still rotting, stomp it out before it ghosts.

In the End, a New Sensation Comes

Because a thousand brilliant lights yes

    Because the gray abscess of you is this face

Because all glass shine here in tremor folds

    Because I fashion a love so thirsty

Because what we are more than is my mouth fine

    Because you make me want *want*

Because of the jutting and slits of you (parse me)

    Because your arm becomes leg and five bones

Because the smoke out your face holes means (carry me)

    Because if I am understanding you I am free

Because I pick up wind and sand and pelican things

    Because of how I puncture it I will be radiant

Because a penny in the funnel sounds like

I'm decorated

terro

bleeds ou

jars hold m

is a wan

go tilt nov

in the brok

splinterin

in the aliv

move quickl

without yo

and foc

nothing fe

The Forgetting Hole

                    Forgetting in the middle of forgetting
as in the tongue is clipped and trotted off. I forget
where I am going all the time. On the lamb or on
the map while a whole city flocks to sleep, I forget
the kettle on the stove. Boiling, the city shakes its keys
and I forget again the noise that pumps our lungs
full of forgetting cancer. In the smoke that brews
its charge of forgetful things, I forget how forgetting
is easy, its absence forgetting everyday. Forgets needle
in the sober dish like forgetting to inject thoughts
with adjectives. Forget static mayhem across
a tooth-lined street. A city forgets in the name of blood
and harp. What flails me and what floods with joy.
Or beginnings, forgetting those as well. I lap around
but I cannot part from your shoulder cave. To forget you,
I must punch holes in every almanac. You must
forget me too, all the selfish hungers meant only to fill

to forget loneliness trying to forget itself

down the forgetting hole. I pass the many thrills

of forgotten objects. When it storms, your whole

body thunders. I am scared of loud noises, of losing

and leaving. When people leave me, I will have forgotten you.

Evacuation

No you don't live here anymore. This house

is a ship that has parted. When you wake up

from a thousand-year slumber, the world will be

a less content version of its current self. *Or raining fire,*

the mystic says. *There will be men dressed in blisters hobbling*

through the streets like smashed marionettes. Such fury

fuels the house adrift, the house cobwebbed but wanting

of visitors. Though the panels are flailed by leaky

acid and you are sitting there while the burns kiss you

through flesh. Though unnamed creatures with sprawling legs

wrap themselves around each window. Wild

are the spinning hands of a fevered clock

rippling through shingles. Every rumble should

suggest *feel*. Sometimes a hunger moves

through your belly but nothing tears. Evacuate the bones,

let the skin hang dry. A pale flag upon a once body. Uninhabited.

What stillness will love you now: nobody, no one, nothing.

Paradise in a Fevered Dream

At the fat lip edge of the world, there is a blue boat
in cannibal water. Wearing a blue dress, I was confused
for all species of animal and was devoured. You speak

of an insistent love using all seven tentacles. Your eighth
arm somewhere in the belly of a white whale. Though odd
limbed, you row with such diligence. My teeth, tiny oars.

Drink so much salt, we bloat and are succulent. I demand
a planet audience during placid hours when tumbling
fire leaps from sky to sky. We kiss and burn and kiss again.

Shall we grieve today? How we begin our mornings. Crack
an egg on your pretty head and let the tadpoles suck
the runny yolk. I wake up everyday thinking I am dead.

Then check: Can I fasten myself to ledge like a barnacle?
Is my mouth a prison of gilded words? If you touch
my scales, will I turn fish and sacrifice? The rest of the day

spent in silence. You go hungry. You go wan and peck
at fish bone and peel. I offer you trout and sticky
fingers. I offer you my grim pouch and so-so knuckle

of flesh. If not for loneliness, you would unhinge your jaw
and gorge. To the gulls, we are bricolage of scrap metal
and fruit pit, not enough meat to tender though we

welcome each slice of flying debris overhead. Pleased
to find our ribs good and strong today. We are optimistic
for the future even if flesh begins as tomb, ends as tomb.

Promenade in a City of Ghosts

And my eyes descend into an imagined color.

The sky is often confused with ash.

I know less and less about this world.

This city that rains for years without stop.

Now I wait in rituals of sleep.

Each night, I return to you with a pocket of jasmine.

We walk side by side, more ghost than ghosts.

We pause for red: a siren, poinsettia, bodega light.

After death, you appreciate these brief pleasures.

I am swollen with sound, humming.

We arrive at last. Your dead body glistens under a pointed milk light. In a white basin, I clean you with pink salt and a lithe tongue. I taste the willow and coriander supple of your unholy dead upon dead. I brush the wicked from your tangled hairs. Your say-nothing mouth watches and turns mirror in the spittle. You turn flock and disappear.

I want noise. I want the heart. I want each center slowly moving. The mouth to inflate. A hand to feel like a hand. I want to love like this in a living city.

IN ABSENTIA-LAND:

A WEDDING

In Absentia-land, my lover is granulated and chockfull of paper bombs. Such confetti love I hardly knew. I read a book on specters that taught me how to move: *ash quickly.* Say this with authority so the leap is not so great. *What is the name for flesh again? I forget.* Another thing: skin is unreliable as paperweight. The music is ambient at the bar when we slink in. A whiskey gash and glitter shrapnel. Through some clever talk, I am convinced freedom is a skill we learn through proper upkeep. When we smash into each other that same night—all our ghoulish fingers into every hole—then a galaxy worth of spill.

How to Live through a Mobile Terror

The sun rises hacked in center. There is hope
to channel and like melon seeds—to burst

is no ordinary act. All thirsty believers, marching
dote on this violence. To live through this, carry

a great necro-thorn and shun the molten spews
from red rubbed skies. For fanged delinquents

of these future days, make the belly bloat
and meaty in preparation for unbearable noise.

What sweeps the dust and sparks hexes and spoils.
All will be good in time. Grass tethered to people,

people tethered to wick to air so thick with animal
grief—we wear its tendons like the blackest of veils.

Notes on After-World Matrimony

So watch me closely through the narrow gates

of after-world hell. This bone-lake gathering

algae and medley of human jowls.

*

On the state of carnival debris: when I walk

with you hand in hand, peel apart. Eager

to wed you with charred lace snagged

against brick and spew flower.

*

I saw that the sun was awry and then it was

purple and smoke. I saw the days of you

in the sick of a chewed palm thrust through drywall.

*

When I am on the surgical table waiting to be cut

then threaded, I want to remember the color of my blood.

*

This cake means you chose me. Why we have each guest

bring flour and chardonnay—to bake and to hope.

*

I hope you will hold tarp over me while the earth

topples over. I will build you a tall house

on elastic stilts and teach us to overcome vertigo.

*

When injury becomes extinct, this is how

we know death repeats itself. We line

our boxes with silk, make ourselves comfortable.

Fall into all kinds of disaster bliss.

We—an After-World Anthem

Foliage of people in an endless parade: make it mean something.

Blinked passages of time in accelerated speed.

You in a glass tube shot back to metropolis.

Me in a ghost cab still on hold with Verizon.

The window to our destiny somewhere between shellac and a cold compress.

*

Say something meaningful everyday.

I am on hold with you while the face of the city is turning.

Drones litter pieces of you like confetti.

I am full of holes and government rations.

*

The carnival whirl of intimacy in the age of hyphens.

My love for my country full of jelly.

My love splintered and sung by funereal pomp.

A procession led by the unctuous dead all dressed in lacquered bones.

Send us to farther lunarscapes so we can better pray.

Send me a phone bill tall as the last skyscraper remade as vertical tomb.

Whatever pockmark of the skull shines through.

*

We're half wool, half tyrant.

Our living is hackneyed, forged of tiny prickly houses and their even tinier shoes.

I am combusting in the backseat waiting for the next available representative.

My spine now loosed and without a country.

Wave to the people in their assorted fugue states.

May we be forever parsed across a spectrum of names.

We Become Good Seers

Cowed flower procession:
note how a clown bites
the flower's edge. See tear
gas and people rally from
stem to stem. We say

coexistence and *resistance*.
In the name of revolution,
I lay my head against
your head. Within my narrow
corridors I worship black
boots and stampedes.
Do not mean to idealize

weight of being
trampled. I mean
protection or pressed

against you, pulp

to pulp. Squeeze of limbs.

Need and fright. We vein

and coil. We thirst—

are rewarded for

our thirst. Choose

to believe you love me

through wither and reborn;

are deliberate in our union.

Vine kissed against vine

and veil. When I open,

I become red

planet and air chokes.

Surprised to find

you rippling beneath

my flesh, planning

a new city. Not sure how

to love or fear you

but choose again to believe

love—not a sieve

but an archive grown into

muscle remembering everything.

Future Song

Darling death brigade. So effortless
in their gummy black. Grave
distance of a sober hankering for—

(comfort me)

When I spy body, I spy rot.
We have come so far to shimmy
at the root (and mind the dark)

(comfort me)

Purpling bodies full of salt.
So I will sew so deeply into you.
I will skylight fracture and closer
to bobble head feeling

(comfort me)

Kiss me, oblong forward. Without

the hazard mask. Let the world take

bone shape. Let it go quick into the acid

drop and should it keel—

(eradicate me)

The Lost Years

Clot in the breaking room, so I am forgotten.

The terror yields in threefold. One is miracle web. The second—twine.

The dancer pirouettes onto a bed of knives.

As a doll thing. Everything misheard.

The house is a meadow is painted yellow over black.

Spotted ghost in the mirror parts my hair with turpentine and a swallow brush.

Taupe confusion. A lilac in the room imitates a scream.

Open your mouth your glass container of half truths. All that cherry mayhem.

MOURN YOU BETTER

Abstraction muse: let us not do this anymore.

I pluck. You pluck. I grieve. You wisp and billow

in the spectral air, and a rotting sneaks my way.

Tilt happens and you dutifully haunt the thistle space

with the *dead* dead of it, save for some brief

memory of salt and emergency piston.

I would tamper with all the tinker bodies, unscrew

the screws to let the eyes drown in that milkweed

version of better mourning.

Mourn you better. I am so good at saying the thing,

the generous hole and ballooning throat. Somber

and wiser and brimming over the row of slender boxes.

I can taste the skull shine and the skin batter.

I can mew and claw at the tendril space between lungs.

I am going about my day with pomp and the most brilliant noise
I am disco-praying to ambient gods and mirror floors.

Only sometimes do I think of the way you touch.

Touch: A Recovery Project

Touch acknowledges cavity in chest center. Touch should in theory be essentially good for knowing salt and gravity.

Touch is akin to knowing flesh and knowing flesh is—I know it when the follicle stings that my heart has turned the way of glass.

I know that touch is what bludgeons. I know what shuts itself in the mouth and threatens to rust through the gulp down. I know what sews itself to flesh in such a way that flesh no longer recognizes flesh. I know what flesh must do to preserve the sanctity of touch so that *to be touched* means *to be touched*, and only just that.

Touch to finger the splitting harp. Touch to know the wreck that brews within me and phantoms of my nodding noose. Touch made of red sharps, feral and bleak. Touch me in the flint of a blank corridor when the world heaves into many bends—let it funnel into fever.

Museum of Dead Lovers

Touch is some other life's remedy for sickly thoughts.

The filaments of time buckling over with rose gold mourning.

Two lovers dead—dead in mouth and corpse-eye dead.

*

See how the mobile turns in lovers' awning.

A phone conversation transcribed onto tablet of blanks.

Hiss in the corner and when one strokes the other's hair—

Twin statics projected onto a white wall.

Molars in carousel lights—the kiss that was tongue-touched.

*

I remember this well—dream a dream of me in stones.

Docent this clattering of bones behind plaque and velvet rope.

There was union and then there was not.

And it was nobody's fault.

*

See how with flagrant torch these lovers wanted the world.

The stain of two oils moving towards the obscene.

One day this trap will know how scents keep and we will never be left wondering.

Consulting the Bones

Surveyor, take note of this happy reunion: pelvis

finds biological torso. Absent years and then this peculiar find.

The return after continental slips. Thin lives punctuated in transit.

One grew a second tongue. Flesh lost to labor, the other.

They have known cold machines. Promises of gold, anchorage,

sweet morsels of God. Their parts unwilling

to fit, will not lock in gaps and jutted wings. Wholeness

was never made for enduring bodies. We have buried

too many of them. Rickety homes, newborn

mouth wide as entrance. Beyond one terminal is another.

Soon, one forgets the taste of sky. There are only small

pleasures now: floor to kneel, one anthem, engorged tit.

Reason to want. There is fatigue in this history,

and passing. There is repetition and passing.

Happiness Theorem

Attempting to write this while bearing witness to the possibility of joy in a more miraculous plane. Sometimes the spools of our words shoulder a responsibility to this joy making. The conundrum being, in these instances, that joy is never a given. It is founded upon disappointment. Who or what has disappointed you lately? Disappointment is a close cousin to treason, which is an irrational feeling in the body that assails against its own organs. What we strive for should be a circulatory effort in which treason does not linger at the spleen but rather filters through towards a more useful feeling. Since we are taught to look upon gestures of utility with blanket approval, we can only assume that this is objectively a good thing. The pragmatism of happiness like a row of bobbins in color order. The image relinquishes the improbable, which is luck running up the storm drain. To insist on the determinant quality of fortune is to deny that we can be both problem and solution. Problem: happiness like a whisker light bled into dark. Solution: wed the animals of the dark to better learn their language. This is why we invest in prayer. This is why we pray so heavily for stacks upon stacks of ordinary feeling and do things with such care.

How to Find Each Other in the Dark

Of fine-in-the-hole—opt not

to mallet. Instead want

the body good even if so

weary. Sense numbed

or combed over with

forgetting. This hook

on flesh is what cuts

through paper. Split open

that difficult nut. Fill it

with yellow. It is

a flower—no, it is

a weed. One means more

beautiful but feral is

the other so be terror

blossom and wild. Be

tender too, however

knobbed the notion.

The lesson: grope

for each other

in the dark, even if light

scarce because dark

is neither good nor

bad, though sometimes

we live in the month of

the bad. Let us simmer

in the difference, in error

and affliction. If there is

fail-sound, then

fine. If there is prick

in the chest—fine. I am

a lantern. You are a lantern.

Directions for a Better Life

Or *simply you would complete me*,

the sinewy voice milks the trees and ornery

blossoms. What you say next—I am red

in the face. I will and can harp on a spleen.

In the sidelines of a purple desert, a mote

erects itself between dashboard

and a vein. Sometimes I believe

in the virtues of a robotic dusk. I believe in

dirty thoughts and my gummy hands going

this way and then that. *Are you feeling*

better now? Good. Rest your pretty head

on a briar patch. Sweet nothings. I think

when I whisper, someone is pushing

a button and saying, *Now move into*

the happily before they take down the sun

and so I take her hand and pulse hard

into the forever-morgue. *My darling,*

I will go wherever you go.

Creation Myth

At first, we wander through the arid stretch. Somewhere between chaos and the beginning of human life. The sky is gaseous swarms of a suspended pink. We are inside it, weaving through its thin veils. In each corner of this world, a gnarled root grows anywhere but down. There is the company of sand, chattering teeth of water lap. A god of fossil and molten preserves. We walk with every bone rattling inside us. The vanishing point obscured by the squint. There are no names for this. We flex our mouths, examining its open and limits. To be capable of contortions and uncontained sound. The sky buckles with fire and star debris. Each illuminated fall telling us: *Run!*

IN ABSENTIA-LAND:

AN EPILOGUE

Premonition

On a red order, I go and examine the provenance

       of all things. There is the looming god-hand. Clarity

of smoke. Children pelting across a lawn of slow grass.

       The sprinklers are running still. The clocks drone on.

The end is near. There are warts that know the sun

       is turning black. Their growth half-thwarted. I want

the best unravel for you and I even as tide folds over

       everything. The city will catch in flames and grow new

and polished. There will not be a second discovery

       of fire, no newness on my back. I am good using my two

able hands. There should be some cause for alarm. I know

       someone up there will punish us with planetary fury for this—

A version of a story as lovely and cumbersome as this cries out *Mourn and mourn me!* How people people this space. Their endless mounds of flesh. In the terminal, we watch the tarmac light up with attendants holding lanterns. Someone calls these *bouquets of hope* and we laugh because *how quaint.* Though you come back to me. We look out into the distance where there are no flowers. There are planes needling into sky and sky blasting open. There is an ellipsis in the sky. There are no flowers. You say, *Yes, bouquets of hope.* Something to wear upon our persons, which are prone to splinter and discord, jutting every which way.

Museum of the Lost City

See city in after-world confetti in its most pixelated year.

Terror everywhere in billboards and storming marquees.

In Absentia-land—reliable in ghost ash upkeep.

See this skeletal shrapnel and infinite glass.

The world in lost towers and country shells.

People too, hanging on a fish line.

You would think, some authority over flesh, but no—

In the pages that burn, fail utterances of *I, you, me, us.*

There were white birds singed in the sky.

There were paper and noise and people in the sky.

Memory frayed, everything frayed.

No longer a viable space for feeling but then came the mourn.

See city so lovely and lonely in its after-after—just a little bit touched.

ACKNOWLEDGEMENTS

Poems in this book have appeared in the following publications:

"Directions for a Better Life" – Kundiman's "Fireside: A Kundiman Blog"

"Evacuation" – *Rogue Agent*

"Garden of Perennial Things" and "Dead Things" – *Barzakh*

"Happiness Theorem" – *Jellyfish Magazine*

"Hologram Theory" – *NOÖ Journal*

"How to Find Each Other in the Dark," "Consulting the Bones," and "Museum of Dead Lovers" – Kelsey Street Press' blog

"I Love You, Dead" – Birds of Lace's "30 x Lace"

"In Absentia-land, we become two tiny terrors…" – *Gigantic Sequins*

"Misery Machine," "Touch: A Recovery Project," and "We Become Good Seers" – *Twelfth House*

An excerpt from "MOURN YOU BETTER" – *Ghost Proposal*

"Notes on After-World Matrimony" – *dusie*

"Robot Pleasure" – *inter|rupture*

Muriel Leung is from Queens, New York. Her writing can be found or is forthcoming in *The Collagist*, *Fairy Tale Review*, *Ghost Proposal*, *Jellyfish Magazine*, *inter|rupture*, and others. She is a recipient of a Kundiman fellowship and is a regular contributor to The Blood-Jet Writing Hour poetry podcast. She also edits poetry for *Apogee Journal*. Currently, she is pursuing her PhD in Creative Writing and Literature at University of Southern California.